MUSH
ROOM
MAGIC

AN ILLUSTRATED INTRODUCTION
TO FASCINATING FUNGI

DR SAPPHIRE MCMULLAN-FISHER
ILLUSTRATIONS BY MARTA ZAFRA

**Smith
Street
Books**

CONTENTS

18
THE
MUSHROOMS

INTRODUCTION ─────────────●

Have you ever marveled at a fairy ring that appeared in your backyard, seemingly overnight? What about a massive mushroom colony you stumbled across while walking in the woods? Or perhaps you have fond memories of a meal filled with delicious foraged fungi? If you've ever been amazed by mushrooms, then this book is for you.

Whenever you admire a mushroom growing on the forest floor or reach for a handful from the supermarket produce section, you're in the presence of an ancient lifeform, evolved from the fungi that inhabited the Earth millions of years ago. Today, scientists contend that there are likely more than 100,000 different fungi species, yet an estimated 95 percent remain unidentified, waiting to be discovered.

Parsing through those species, the sheer variety of shapes, sizes, colors, scents, and textures proves that nature is indeed the world's greatest artist. From cream to magenta, deep purple, and inky-black, the kaleidoscopic hues of mushrooms are beautiful to behold. Then there's the variety of forms fungi take: Look closely and you'll see parasols, fans, trumpets, and many other strange shapes. We've included some of the most distinct and memorable mushrooms in this book, but there are many, many more out there – and even more yet to be officially identified and classified.

This book is based on available scientific data and ethnomycology at the time of publication. Good science will change and build on knowledge. Our understanding of mushrooms comes from millennia of exploration by Indigenous peoples and their care of the natural world. We would like to recognize and respect the work of all contributors to our collective understanding.

Even though there is still so much to learn about mushrooms, there's a wealth of existing knowledge to soak up. We hope this book sparks a lifelong love of mushrooms and other fungi. May their captivating magic excite, delight, and intrigue you, as it has for the legions of others mushroom lovers among us.

THE MANY ROLES OF MUSHROOMS

Mushrooms are essential to our ecosystems. They provide sustenance to many species, including rabbits, squirrels, bears, and deer, as well as a huge number of insects that rely on fungi as a food source. Through invisible, underground networks, some mushrooms help surrounding plants to thrive; they are a key factor in soil biodiversity, and the Earth's forests, fields, and farms couldn't survive without them.

Quite the multitaskers, mushrooms play an important role beyond the natural environment, utilized by humans in a variety of ways. They are a key ingredient in most antibiotics, cholesterol-reducing medication, vegan leather alternatives, natural fabric dyes, soothing balms, psychological treatment alternatives, Indigenous cultural ceremonial potions, and even emerging sustainable building materials. Is there anything mushrooms can't do?

But above all else, most of us associate mushrooms with eating. From the delicious saffron milkcap to the ubiquitous oyster mushroom and the prized golden chanterelle, most foodies would agree that the culinary world just would not be the same without the humble mushroom. Pickled, dried, fried, roasted, boiled, or even eaten raw, they are enjoyed a multitude of different ways by people from all over the world, every day. Whether building the base of a Japanese broth or appearing on a Spanish tapas menu, mushrooms are kitchen heroes to home cooks and celebrated chefs alike.

MUSHROOMS AS CULTURAL TOUCHSTONES

Mushrooms have captured the imaginations of many artists and creators around the world. Appearing in iconic video games, playful children's stories, classic cartoons, terrifying television series, and beyond, mushrooms have ridden many trends over time. They have been represented as everything from hypnotic to menacing, with countless written and illustrated representations throughout the ages.

A variety of meanings can be attributed to mushrooms, depending on who you ask: They are a recurring element in the folklore and mythology of many cultures. Some believe they symbolize death, while others associate them with magic, luck, and longevity.

Some Indigenous communities around the world consider mushrooms to be both a powerful form of medicine and a mystical conduit to the spiritual world. Using mushrooms in healing rituals is a significant (and sacred) act that Indigenous people have taken part in for centuries.

In the 1960s, psychologists advocated for the use of "magic mushrooms," but their research was halted due to governmental intervention: It was several decades before Western medicine began to recognize and embrace the healing potential of fungi again. Today, many people still associate psychedelic mushrooms with the '60s – a time when a new wave of music, art, and literature flourished as creators opened their minds to new experiences.

Fungi are an ancient lifeform, but our collective fascination with unravelling their many mysteries shows no sign of ebbing. In fact, interest in mycology only appears to be accelerating as we find out more. As long as mushrooms exist, there will be someone studying, photographing, painting, drawing, and sculpting them, just as other creators have done for centuries.

FINDING FUNGI IN THE WILD

All around the world, you'll find mushrooms sold by suburban supermarkets, upmarket providores, open-air farmers' markets, roadside food stalls, and straight from the growers at rural farm gates. Of course, some of us choose to skip the middleman and head out into the forest to forage for ourselves.

Then there are people who go in search of mushrooms, not to eat, but to admire. Pretty, fan-shaped cinnabar oysterlings are always a delight to behold, while the red, spotted cap of the fly agaric elicits a smile from anyone who has ever read a fairytale. By night, those lucky enough to spot the eerie glow of bioluminescent species know how special it is to witness this mysterious phenomenon.

However, while mushroom appreciation is admirable, it is equally important to remember the fragility of the natural world. Sadly, many species are in a vulnerable position due to deforestation, climate change, and unsustainable foraging practices. With this in mind, it's important to tread carefully while searching for mushrooms and to be mindful of the threats fungi face. When hiking and foraging, take only what you need and be mindful of not spreading pathogens via your boots and gear.

NOTES ON SAFE & ETHICAL FORAGING

It's exciting to head out into nature to find different fungi, but you should always practice caution when foraging. While we provide information on some of the identifying characteristics of each mushroom, this is only intended as a means to develop your understanding and should never be used for real-world identification.

It may be mighty tempting to collect and cook a bounty of mushrooms you stumble across while walking through your local woodlands, but you should never eat a mushroom based solely on what you've read in books or online. Instead, learn from experienced people in your local area. Find out how to identify "look alikes" (as well as the mushrooms you are foraging for) so you can spot the differences between species with confidence. If you're even slightly unsure if you should eat a mushroom found in the wild, that's a sign to leave it uneaten.

Generally, many mushrooms are inedible without being poisonous, but unfortunately some are toxic. Deadly species have been described as delicious, so taste, smell, and other characteristics (like peeling or reaction to silver) should never be relied upon. The consequences of eating the wrong mushrooms are serious (and sometimes fatal), so taking risks isn't wise.

When you're foraging, be a good human and think about the delicate ecosystem you're a part of. Don't take more than you can eat, process, or refrigerate for a few days. Mushrooms go off and rot – if they look bad don't eat them. Be sure to leave older mushrooms to spread their spores and provide sustenance for the many different species of animals that also rely on fungi for nourishment.

USEFUL TERMS ────────────────────────●

Biotrophic
Relating to an organism that draws essential nutrients from its host to live. This relationship may be benificial, neutral, or parasitic depending on circumstances.

Bryophytes
The collective term for mosses, liverworts, and hornworts. These small plants reproduce via spores rather than seeds.

Decomposer
A type of fungus that decomposes organic materials like wood and leaf litter to get its energy. These mushrooms are important in the recycling of nutrients in ecosystems.

Edible
Fungi that have been eaten by local people and do not contain any known toxins.

Fibrils & fibrillose
Fiber- or hair-like structures, these may cover a surface (usually on the cap or stem) resulting in a hairy or furry appearance.

Inedible
Inedible mushrooms should not be eaten, as it is unknown what compounds they contain.

Medicinal
Medicinal fungi are known to have beneficial therapeutic and/or nutritional benefits.

Milk
A milky liquid some fungi exude when they are cut or torn – some species have much more than others.

Mycorrhizal
A type of fungus with beneficial symbiotic relationships with the roots of plants. The fungus partner shares nutrients and water from the soil and the plant shares sugars from photosynthesis.

Parasitic
Parasitic fungi live off other organisms. There is no benefit to the host, which can become unhealthy, but these relationships can often be stable for decades to centuries.

Phenols & phenolic odor
Phenols are a class of organic compounds that emit a distinctly sweet, tarry smell.

Psychoactive
Psychoactive fungi have the principal active compounds psilocybin and psilocin, which cause psychedelic effects if consumed.

Short-gills
These are shorter gills that may be interspersed between the gills that reach from the stem to the margin. These may be regularly or irregularly arranged depending on the species.

Spore Print
The process used to collect a deposit of spores to determine the spore color. This is a key feature used for identifying mushrooms.

Striate
Distinct lines, often roughly parallel. Used to describe features on the cap margin or stem.

Toxic
Toxic fungi contain compounds that are poisonous. Some can be deadly.

Umbo & umbonate
An umbo is a raised bump or protrusion in the middle of a mushroom cap. Caps with this feature are described as umbonate.

Universal veil
A membrane that encloses some species as they form. As the fungus matures, the veil detaches. Remnants may be present as a sack on the stem base or as patches on the cap.

MUSHROOM ANATOMY

Cap

Also referred to as a pileus, this upper part of a mushroom is the easiest to spot. The cap contains and protects the spore-producing structures. Its color, shape, and texture indicates a mushroom's stage of development.

Gills

Often located on the cap's underside, gills produce and release spores. Their patterns are key to mushroom identification. Easily identifiable characteristics include how they attach to the stem (stem attachment), color, spacing, length, and forking. Not all fungi have gills.

Margin

The edge of a mushroom's cap. Margins can be striate, grooved, scalloped, wavy, inrolled, or upturned. They are used to identify age, and for studying the interaction between a mushroom and its environment.

Mycelium

Mycelium are made up of hyphae – thread-like, tubular filaments that form a mass. These are present at the base of the stem, where they are bundled together or interwoven in a mat of threads. Most mycelium are microscopic and limited in scope, but some networks cover square miles – the largest organisms in the world, which can live for millennia. Mycelium perform multiple functions, including the provision of nutrients, protection, and communication between fungi and plants.

Pores

While mushrooms most often have gills, some have pores on the underside of their caps. These small holes are the base of tubes running inside the cap; they allow spores to escape into the environment.

Ring

Located on the stem of some fungi, a ring, or annulus, is the remnant of a partial veil; as the mushroom grows, this veil, which stretches from the cap to the stem, detaches, and its remnant forms a ring.

Sack

A cup-like structure at the base of a mushroom, the sack is the remnant of the universal veil. Also called a volva.

Stem

Also called a stipe, the stem supports the cap and elevates it into a suitable position for spore distribution.

Spores

Fungi's main reproduction mechanism, similar to seeds, released from gills or pores.

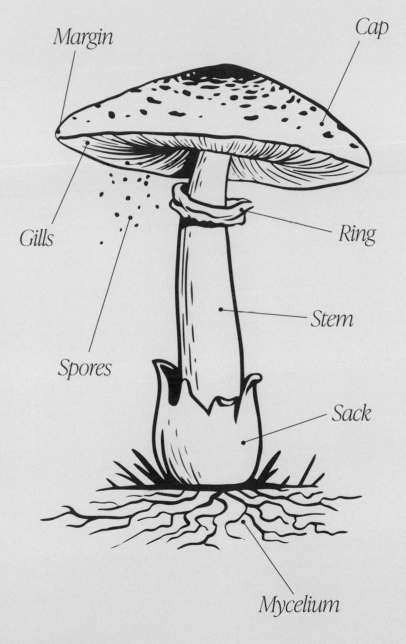

Margin

Cap

Gills

Ring

Spores

Stem

Sack

Mycelium

CAP SHAPES

Aside from color, the shape of a mushroom's cap is often one of its most obvious features. In some species, the shape of a cap changes as the mushroom matures.

Campanulate
The cap is bell shaped.

Conical
The cap is cone shaped.

Convex
The cap is rounded, like an upside-down bowl.

Cylindric
The cap is cylinder shaped and tall.

Depressed
The cap dips in the middle.

Infundibuliform
The cap is funnel shaped.

Ovoid
The cap is egg shaped.

Papillate
The cap has a small, rounded umbo – see umbonate.

Parabolic
The cap is cylinder shaped and short.

Plane
The cap is flat.

Umbilicate
The cap has a small dip in the middle.

Umbonate
The cap has an umbo – a raised bump or protrusion in its middle.

TYPES OF STEM ATTACHMENT ⟶

Stem attachment describes how a mushroom's gills attach to its stem. Some gills are free and don't attach to the stem at all, while others are decurrent and extend down the stem.

Adnate
The entire width of the gills attaches to the stem.

Adnexed
The gills slope upward before attaching to the stem.

Collared
The gills attach to a collar that encircles the stem.

Decurrent
The gills extend down the stem.

Emarginate
The gills are notched before attaching to the stem.

Free
The gills do not attach to the stem.

Sinuate
The gills are notched before attaching to the stem and extending slightly down.

Subdecurrent
The gills extend slightly down the stem.

THE
MUSHR

BROWN ROLL-RIM

Paxillus involutus

These mottled brown mushrooms, found in woodlands, parks, and gardens, can blend in to their habitat so well that they're easy to trip over. Although you might be tempted to eat these innocuous-looking mushrooms, this common species is toxic and should be treated with caution. Not convinced? In the 1940s, renowned German mycologist Julius Schaeffer died from cumulative toxicity after consuming dishes prepared with brown roll-rims, becoming the only professional mycologist known to have died from eating poisonous mushrooms.

APPEARANCE
These medium-sized, mottled mushrooms are often sticky when wet and darken when bruised or mature. The caps are convex when young, then become funnel-shaped with a depressed center and pronounced, in-rolled rim. The caps are brown, with tints that include red-, yellow-, and olive-browns. The gills are decurrent and forked, brownish-yellow and relatively thick and crowded, sometimes becoming pore-like near the stem. The spore print is brown. The stems are central, robust, and often misshapen and tapered toward the base.

GROWTH
This mycorrhizal mushroom appears after rain from late summer through fall in temperate deciduous and coniferous woods. Widely distributed across the northern hemisphere, this species has inadvertently been introduced to Australia, New Zealand, South Africa, and throughout South America, probably transported in soil with the European trees it partners with.

NOTES
Despite being widely eaten throughout Central and Eastern Europe, this mushroom can cause gastric upsets when eaten raw. It has recently been found to cause a potentially fatal autoimmune disorder, even in people who have previously consumed the mushroom without any other ill effects.

Clumps of these magnificent mushrooms can be found on dead tree stumps and rotting wood throughout temperate regions of North America, Asia, and Europe. This species is best known for forming large, long-lived colonies that sometimes become small-town tourist attractions. These huge fungi, known as "humongous fungus," cover miles of territory, weigh thousands of pounds, and have been dated as thousands of years old. Crystal Falls, Michigan, holds an annual Humongous Fungus Fest to celebrate its colossal colony.

APPEARANCE

These mushroom clumps typically have swollen stem bases. They start with veils on the caps, which protect the gills when young. The caps begin convex with furry, fine scales and in-rolled margins, becoming flat with an umbo as they mature; their colors vary from yellow-brown to red-brown and fade with drying. The gills are crowded and adnate or weakly decurrent; initially almost white, they become yellowish-brown with age. The spore print is white, and the stems are central. An extensive system of black, root-like structures called rhizomorphs may be present.

GROWTH

An ecologically important wood-decay fungus, this mushroom lives as a decomposer or opportunistic parasite in weakened tree hosts. It is most common on the dead stumps and buried, rotting wood of broad-leafed trees and conifers.

NOTES

The mycelium of this fungus may be bioluminescent, although it can be tricky to spot the soft, green glow with the naked eye. While these mushrooms are edible, they have been known to cause digestive issues for some people; cooking is recommended.

BULBOUS
HONEY FUNGUS

Armillaria gallica

CHI-NGULU-NGULU

Termitomyces titanicus

Found only on the African continent, the world's largest edible mushroom is farmed by termites in their mounds. These enormous fungi can weigh up to 5.5 lb (2.5 kg), usually appear singly, and are referred to by many names in different African languages. Despite its prevalence in parts of Africa, this impressive fungus wasn't identified by Western scientists until the 1980s.

APPEARANCE

These huge mushrooms have caps that span 15–30 inches (38–76 cm), with a Guinness World Record–breaking specimen reaching a whopping 39 inches (99 cm). The caps are broadly umbonate with variable colors and textures, and sometimes become ridged and cracked with age; they are often creamy to pale brown with a darker center, growing paler toward the margins. The gills are free, crowded, and white or off-white, bruising pink-brown. The stems are tough, central, long, broad, and white to off-white, with a large fleshy ring. The stem bases taper to a distinctive long "root" shape, which is deeply connected to the termite mound below.

GROWTH

This decomposer is found on termite mounds during the early rainy season, from West Africa through the Congo into Southern Africa. Its termite partners rely on harvesting leaves from forests, woodlands, and grasslands, so surrounding vegetation is required for the termite mounds (and fungi) to grow.

NOTES

A delicious mushroom with a meaty texture, this gargantuan fungus is described as having a savory and smoky taste. The stems and tougher specimens can be softened by simmering in milk or boiling in a stew.

This small, bright, fan-like mushroom's distinctive shade really sets it apart. With exquisitely rich coloring, this mushroom glows like a precious red jewel amid the green and brown hues of the forest. Spotting a cinnabar oysterling is a real treat for mushroom lovers lucky enough to stumble across this rare find.

APPEARANCE

This stemless, fan-shaped mushroom is recognizable from its typical, bright orange-red color – particularly on the flame-shaped fibers of the caps and gill margins. The caps are convex and fan shaped with finely scaled or felty textures, particularly when young; at the base, the texture may become bald and dry. The gills are adnexed and crowded with several lengths of short-gills, orderly arranged, starting off pale buff when young and becoming pale brown, with red edges. The spore print is pale brown. Without a true stem, this species often features a velvety, flat pad and is attached laterally to wood. These fungi can fade to a dull creamy buff.

GROWTH

This rare decomposer is scattered across woodlands from late summer to the end of fall. Commonly found in eastern North America, this species also occurs in Central and South America, Asia, and Europe. As the cinnabar oysterling grows on hardwoods, its bright colors make it conspicuous on fallen branches and rotting, dead broad-leafed trees.

NOTES

This uncommon mushroom's great beauty delights and captivates photographers. As a species that lives on wood in the wild, it can be threatened in areas where forests and woodlands are cleared of their branches, logs, trunks, and stumps. It is inedible.

CINNABAR OYSTERLING

Crepidotus cinnabarinus

DEATH CAP

Amanita phalloides

With an appropriately grim name, this mycorrhizal species has killed (and not just in fictional murder mysteries): It is responsible for 90 per cent of mushroom-related fatalities around the world. One small death cap contains enough poison to kill an average-sized adult. Usually found near oak trees, these mushrooms sometimes grow in fairy rings on the forest floor. Since this species can be tricky to identify, it's best to steer clear of sampling foraged fungi if you've got any suspicions that death caps might be about.

APPEARANCE

These sweet-smelling mushrooms have pale stems with a similarly colored skirt-like ring and a swollen sack toward the base. The caps start hemispherical then become convex and finally flat, with variable colors ranging from pale green to yellow, olive, and sometimes bronze or white; some darker colored caps appear radially mottled. The caps are smooth and sticky when wet. The gills are free, white, and crowded, while the short-gills are unevenly distributed and of various lengths. The spore print is white, and the stem color ranges from white to cream to pale yellow.

GROWTH

The species was originally found across Europe, but accidental introduction to regions in North and South America, Asia, South Africa, Australia, and New Zealand, among others, has occurred with the cultivation of non-native species of oak and chestnut. This species can be found near various broad-leafed trees.

NOTES

These highly toxic mushrooms resemble several edible species, increasing the risk of accidental poisoning, especially as their toxins are resistant to cooking. While death caps are poisonous to most mammals, other animals, like insects and snails, can consume them without being poisoned.

This large mushroom, often a striking orange, is reminiscent of a Halloween jack-o'-lantern. Known for glowing in the dark, this fungus has bioluminescent properties sometimes referred to as "foxfire" in North America. As this toxic species can be mistaken for edible chanterelle, be careful when foraging: Eastern jack o'lanterns should be left in the forest.

APPEARANCE

This species often grows in large clusters. The caps start out convex with a central bump or point, then become flat, with the margins finally irregularly upturned. Smooth and dry, the caps range from bright orange and yellow-orange to orange-brown. The gills are decurrent and close, with tidy short-gills that are orange to yellow-orange. The spore print is creamy white. The stems, pale orange to tan in color, are smooth, dry, robust, and thick; they taper to their base, which is often attached to other mushrooms.

GROWTH

Found from eastern North America into northern Central America, these mushrooms commonly grow on stumps and buried roots from summer to late fall. These decomposers can be opportunistic parasites of hardwoods, often indicating poor tree health.

NOTES

The gills of these mushrooms can sometimes glow in the dark. Not to be eaten, these mushrooms cause vomiting, cramps, and diarrhea when ingested. While research is underway on their apparent antitumor and antibiotic properties, these mushrooms are highly toxic, which means they have no therapeutic value in their natural form.

EASTERN JACK O'LANTERN

Omphalotus illudens

FAWN
CHANTERELLE

Cantharellus isabellinus

These small, brown chantarelles blend in with the floor of their tropical rainforest home. Only found in pockets of Central Africa, where it proliferates after periods of heavy rain, this species is not currently at risk, according to conservation assessments. However, habitat destruction in the form of logging, mining, and land clearing for agriculture represents a threat.

APPEARANCE

These funnel-shaped, slightly acrid-smelling brown mushrooms are found alone or in small groups. The caps range from convex to funnel shaped, often with irregular margins, while the fleshy center can be depressed, with distinct woolly fibers. The pale, pinkish-orange gills are widely spaced, strongly decurrent, and sometimes forked. Between the gills, the species is sometimes weakly veined. The spore print is pale ochraceous pink. The stems are central, cylindrical, and slightly hairy on their upper part, with colors ranging from whitish to dirty tan, becoming yellowish-gray with age; the flesh is solid, slightly widening at the base, with bright orange mycelium.

GROWTH

These tropical chanterelles can be found during the wet season in Cameroon and the Democratic Republic of the Congo, yet may be more widespread throughout Central Africa. This fungus is thought to be a mycorrhizal associate of the dominant tree species of the Guineo-Congolian rainforests.

NOTES

These mushrooms are inedible. The strong and durable timber from the limbali trees associated with these mushrooms is used for construction.

This bright yellow, dainty mushroom is commonly found in the soil of pot plants in homes, backyards, and greenhouses throughout Europe, North America, Australia, and beyond. This pretty little mushroom thrives in wet conditions and is considered beneficial to plants, as it supports their access to vital nutrients, though it is poisonous to consume.

APPEARANCE

These mushroom have caps that are dry and cylindrical or egg shaped when young, changing from bell shaped to broadly conical to flat with a central bump as they age. The caps are bright to pale yellow, fading as they mature, and are often covered with grainy fragments or brown scales concentrated at the center. The crowded gills are free, thin, and yellow. The spore print is white, and the stems are central, long, and even, with a slightly swollen base that may have pale yellow mycelium. Sometimes a fragile ring is also present.

GROWTH

This mushroom can be found after rain all year round, but especially during warmer months. Common across tropical, subtropical, and warmer parts of temperate zones, this mushroom appears in greenhouses or in the pots of indoor plants in cooler regions.

NOTES

This species may improve soil quality, as it can help to break down organic matter (like compost or potting mixture) and provide nutrients for plants. The appearance of this mushroom may indicate overwatering of pot plants, as the species needs moisture to thrive.

FLOWERPOT
PARASOL

Leucocoprinus birnbaumii

FLY AGARIC

Amanita muscaria

This iconic mushroom's red cap with white dots makes it one of the most recognizable mushrooms in the world. A bit of a pop culture icon, this fantastical fungus features in children's cartoons and fairy-tale books, commonly depicted alongside gnomes, fairies, and other whimsical creatures. More recently, this species has been referred to as the "Mario mushroom" for its similarity to the mushrooms in the Super Mario Bros. video games.

APPEARANCE

These large and conspicuous mycorrhizal mushrooms are commonly found reproducing en masse. The caps are typically red but also sometimes orange to yellow. The gills are free and white in color, as is the spore print. The stems are central and also white, usually tapering toward the gills.

GROWTH

Abundant from fall to winter throughout temperate regions, this species can be found near deciduous and coniferous trees and in pine and birch plantings. It's listed for conservation in Canada and Mexico but is an exotic that is considered weedy in Australia, Chile, and New Zealand.

NOTES

Indigenous communities in Afghanistan and across the northern hemisphere (from Sami in the west through to Siberia in the far east) use this psychoactive mushroom as a ritualized intoxicant. When consumed, this toxic species is harmful to the liver. It has several sub-populations, including Eurasian, Eurasian "subalpine," and North American.

These large mushrooms, found in Australia, cast an eerie green glow within the dark forests they inhabit. Capturing the otherworldly, bioluminescent glimmer of the ghost fungus is popular with nature photographers, many of whom trek into forests after dark to snap these mushrooms' somewhat supernatural aura: a true marvel of the natural world.

APPEARANCE

These medium to large mushrooms are often clustered together. The caps are smooth and dry, and start out as convex with an in-rolled margin and depressed center before becoming funnel shaped with age. Cap colors vary from cream and yellow to brown and dark gray, sometimes with hints of blue. The gills are decurrent and white to cream in color, with orderly short-gills. The spore print is white. The stems are often off-center to nearly lateral and tapered toward the base. Bioluminescence is not a definitive characteristic, as some ghost fungi may not glow at all.

GROWTH

This relatively common mushroom is found on wood after rain in some parts of Australia, its peak season between March and June. A decomposer and opportunistic parasite, this mushroom often infiltrates wood and living trees.

NOTES

These mushrooms produce enough of a bioluminescent show that night tours are often held during peak season. A food source for certain snails, slugs, flies, and other arthropods, they aren't suitable for human consumption, due to their toxicity.

GHOST FUNGUS

Omphalotus nidiformis

GOLDEN CHANTERELLE

Cantharellus cibarius

These prized golden mushrooms are highly sought after by foragers. Considered one of the greatest gourmet mushrooms found in the wild, the golden chanterelle's versatility means it can be sauteed, roasted, dried, and pickled. Commercial cultivation of this species has not proven possible, so fungi-loving foodies pay top dollar for these mushrooms when they're sold seasonally by foragers at food markets.

APPEARANCE

These edible, funnel-shaped mushrooms range from light yellow to deep egg yolk in color. The caps are smooth, dry, and flat to upturned at the margins, which can be wavy and in-rolled when young. Red spots will appear on the caps when they are damaged. The gills are wrinkly veins that are decurrent and thick, and may be forked or sinuous near the margins. The spore print is cream to yellow. This species has a faint aroma and flavor of apricots.

GROWTH

These summer mushrooms can also be found into fall and winter in warmer climates after significant rainfall. Growing mainly in deciduous and sometimes coniferous forests, these mycorrhizal fungi are commonly found with oak, chestnut, or hazel trees, from European temperate to subpolar areas, including the Mediterranean, the Balkans, and Scandinavia. The same name has been used in North America and Asia, but research has discovered that the mushrooms growing in those regions are different species. Conservation assessments indicate the golden chanterelle is in decline in some areas, due to industrial pollution and farming additives.

NOTES

This warmly colored species' rich, fruity aroma and flavor make it a popular culinary delight. It's best lightly cooked but possesses enough flavor to carry omelets or rice dishes.

Golden clusters of these edible mushrooms are collected in the wild and cultivated by farmers. Resembling bursts of sunshine, this species is sometimes referred to as a "dashi mushroom" due to the umami it brings to dishes like miso soup. Easily grown on substances like sugar cane mulch, straw, wood, and coffee grounds, it is relatively easy to cultivate at home, especially if you can get your hands on a grow kit.

APPEARANCE

Growing in clusters, these asymmetric, fan-shaped mushrooms feature bright yellow to golden-brown caps, decurrent gills, and reduced stems. The caps are convex and dry, with a fine velvety texture. The gills are white, and closely spaced, with tidy short-gills. The spore print is white. The stems are often fused as part of the cluster. Other mushroom species that appear similar may be toxic.

GROWTH

This decomposer most commonly decays hardwoods such as elm. Naturally occurring in Asia (particularly northern China, Japan, and eastern Russia), this species has been introduced through cultivation to North America, Europe, and beyond.

NOTES

With a complex and aromatic flavor, these gourmet mushrooms are both collected and commercially cultivated, typically grown on grain, sawdust, or straw. An efficient converter of organic materials, the species is a good source of antioxidants and is currently being studied for its ability to decrease blood sugar levels in diabetic mammals.

GOLDEN OYSTER MUSHROOM

Pleurotus citrinopileatus

GOLDEN-SCRUFFY
COLLYBIA

Cyptotrama asprata

This bright orange mushroom is covered in scruffy tufts that look like flames. The golden-scruffy collybia is quite small, but its vibrant color makes it fairly easy to spot in the forests it inhabits. Looking at younger specimens closely, you'll be able to see the tiny spikes that give them a unique mottled texture; if you're hoping to photograph the strange beauty of this mushroom, be sure to take your macro lens to capture a close-up of its remarkable surface.

APPEARANCE

These small mushrooms have caps that are convex or flat and yellow or orange, with younger specimens intensely colored and covered in dense tufts of fibrils that are often lost with age. The margins tend to be rolled inward when young. The orderly gills are adnate or short decurrent, distant, and white to pale yellow. The spore print is white. The stems are central and tapered slightly toward the gills, with the lower areas covered with fine scales or tufts.

GROWTH

Appearing individually or in small colonies, this widely distributed decomposer grows on rotting wood throughout the wet season. It is found on tree stumps, branches, logs, and twigs in wetter forests and rainforests. Found in wet, tropical, subtropical, and temperate regions of the world, this mushroom is absent from Europe and rare in western North America.

NOTES

Small but gorgeous, this brightly colored fungus is a favorite with photographers. While inedible for humans, this mushroom is a food source for slugs and snails, including the endangered rainforest-dwelling camaenid land snail in Australia.

Clusters of these mushrooms may look unassuming during the day, but after the sun sets it's the green pepe's time to shine. Found on branches and logs, this fantastic fungus glows in the dark, bringing a hint of magic to the forests in which it lives. Looking like tiny, green jellyfish floating in an ink-black sea, the bioluminescent beauties are an incredible sight to behold.

APPEARANCE

Clusters of these small mushrooms feature sticky, pale caps that are convex to flat, their colors ranging from pale brownish-gray to buff, these shades darker in the center of the caps. The gills are sometimes adnexed but most often free, with a slight collar and white, orderly short-gills. The spore print is white. The stems are central, smooth, moist, and pale white to grayish in color, with a disc at the base. These mushrooms may emit a strong chemical odor.

GROWTH

Found after rain, this inedible species is a decomposer of woody debris like twigs, branches, and logs. It appears in subtropical and tropical areas of Asia, Australia, and Oceania, though there are recent records of some in South America.

NOTES

Studies have been undertaken to understand the evolution of fungal bioluminescence, which appears to be linked to a single common ancestor from the Cretaceous period. Mushrooms' bioluminescence is due to the production of luciferin in their tissues, although the ecological role of this trait is still a mystery.

GREEN PEPE

Mycena chlorophos

GREEN RUSSULA

Russula virescens

Named "greencracked brittlegill" in some parts of the world, this large mushroom is covered with dark green, angular, cracking patches. Foragers can happily add this edible mushroom to their basket, as its mild flavor makes it a versatile ingredient to cook with when fresh, while when dried, it is suited to broths and soups. Not much of a cook? Simply slice and saute in a little butter to serve alongside a juicy steak.

APPEARANCE

These medium to large mushrooms have dome-shaped caps when young, which become convex to flat with a depressed center with age. The patches on the caps are often angular and vary in density radially around the center, with darker colors ranging from verdigris to grass-green. The flesh between the patches is paler, ranging from creamy to dull yellow, while the gills are white to cream colored and interconnected at their bases by veins. The stems are central and evenly cylindrical; they are typically creamy-white but may discolor to brown with age or handling.

GROWTH

The green russula is found after rains throughout deciduous, mixed forests and tropical, lowland rainforests in Asia, North Africa, Europe, and Central America. As several other species look like this one, its presence in North America and Australia has not yet been clarified, due to taxonomic uncertainty.

NOTES

Considered one of the best edible mushrooms, this versatile mycorrhizal fungus is often sold as a dried product in Asian markets, as drying enhances the nutty flavor. It is commonly used in traditional Chinese medicine, and its enzymes are also employed to break down some dyes used in the textile industry.

These pretty parasols often pop up in meadows as fairy rings. Although this common mushroom is poisonous to humans, it's often mistaken for edible species that look quite similar; found in parks and backyards, it's one of the most misidentified mushrooms, responsible for many poisonings around the world.

APPEARANCE

These medium to large mushrooms have hemispherical or convex caps when young, which become broadly convex or nearly flat with age. Dry and smooth, the caps develop fine fibers and scales, which are concentrated at the center. The gills are free and white when young, usually turning dull green with maturity. The spore print is also dull green. The stems are central, tall, and slightly tapered toward the gills. The stems appear dirty white and may discolor to brown with handling. This species typically bears a double-edged ring that is white on top and brown underneath.

GROWTH

Found after rain from the warmer months into fall, this decomposer grows in lawns, meadows, and pastures. Common in temperate, subtropical, and tropical regions around the world, this mushroom is considered an introduced species in Australia, Cyprus, and the United Kingdom.

NOTES

This poisonous mushroom produces severe gastrointestinal symptoms (such as vomiting and diarrhea). Young children and dogs are at a higher risk of poisoning by this species than adults.

GREEN-SPORED PARASOL

Chlorophyllum molybdites

HALF-DYED
SLENDER CAESAR

Amanita hemibapha

This mushroom's brightly colored red cap makes it stand out like a beacon on the rainforest floor. A highly attractive species, it has graced everything from illustrated children's books to cute embroidery patches, miniature figurines, and even a series of postage stamps released in Papua New Guinea in the 1990s.

APPEARANCE

These medium-sized mushrooms have bright red or orange caps and yellow stems with a ring and a white sack toward the base. The smooth caps are hemispherical when young and become convex to flat, often with a central depression, as they age. The gills start life as creamy-white then become light yellow. The central, yellow stems taper toward the gills and have a skirt-like ring. The bases are white but may have brown patches on the outer surface when young.

GROWTH

This species is found in Asia and Oceania during their wet seasons, although its origin centers in India and Sri Lanka. It is thought to be a mycorrhizal partner of dipterocarp trees in tropical rainforests. Although this name has been widely used, work needs to be done to understand this complex of species.

NOTES

Its beautiful color makes this mushroom a photographer's favorite. There is uncertainty around its edibility, as this species has been recorded as both edible and poisonous, with reported symptoms including dizziness and nausea, particularly if the mushroom is eaten in larger quantities.

These dark, trumpet-shaped mushrooms (often referred to as "black trumpets") are popular in the culinary world. Foragers love hunting for this fungus with its potent, earthy flavor and rich, sweet aroma. These delicious mushrooms are well suited to creamy dishes. As a versatile ingredient, however, horn of plenty can feature on everything from gourmet pizza to humble slices of sourdough toast.

APPEARANCE

These dark, small to medium mushrooms are thin fleshed and pleasant smelling. The cap colors range from gray-black to brown and sometimes yellow-brown. The cap centers are deeply depressed, with felty surfaces, while the stems are hollow. The gills are strongly decurrent, light gray in color, and appear smooth to slightly wrinkled.

GROWTH

This mycorrhizal species can mostly be found with beech, pine, oak, and other broad-leafed trees, on clay- and calcium-rich soils. Found across North America, East Asia, and Europe, these mushrooms have also been recorded in Australia and South Africa, but those sightings may have been of different, similar-looking species.

NOTES

This edible, wild mushroom is prized for its potent, earthy flavor; when dried, it has a black truffle odor. A rich source of protein, horn of plenty also contains polyunsaturated fat, flavonoids, and some ascorbic acid. However, caution is required when consuming these mushrooms, as phenols may also be present. This species is also known as "trumpet of the dead," a reference to the whimsical idea of the mushrooms being played like trumpets by the dead buried beneath them.

HORN
OF PLENTY

Craterellus cornucopioides

HORSE
MUSHROOM

Agaricus arvensis

Associated with manure-enriched pastures, this large, common field mushroom has a global distribution and is sometimes used as an alternative to the portobello mushroom. Whether sauteed, grilled, roasted, or added to stews, the horse mushroom is a hero ingredient in many dishes around the world. While it may not be as well known as some other edible mushrooms, this fungus proves that great things can grow in humble places.

APPEARANCE

Experienced foragers will recognize the cog-wheel pattern on the veil of young specimens of this large, creamy mushroom, which has an odor reminiscent of anise. The whitish, smooth, dry caps start convex then become flat (and potentially brown) with age. The free and crowded gills start out as pink, then become dark chocolate-brown with spore maturity. The stems are central and evenly cylindrical with a small bulb at their base. Caps and stem bases may bruise yellow slowly and without intensity.

GROWTH

Found after heavy rains from late summer to late fall, these common decomposer mushrooms appear in meadows and pastures across Europe, North Africa, Asia, and potentially North America. They are considered introduced in South America, Australia, New Zealand, and Southern Africa. Global conservation assessments consider this species to be of least concern.

NOTES

Although this edible mushroom is productive within well-managed patches fed with plenty of manure, caution is advised, as this species may build up heavy metals in its flesh. Rich in flavor, like most mushrooms, these are best eaten fresh.

This robust mushroom's deep indigo hue and milk make it stand out in the forests where it's found. While a shock of blue may look out of place in the wild and the kitchen, this mushroom is suitable for cooking and eating. Unfortunately, its vibrancy is dulled by cooking, so expect these fungi to turn grayer the longer you cook them. Blue or otherwise, these mushrooms are tasty when pickled or fried.

APPEARANCE

These large, blue mushrooms produce blue milk. The caps have concentric rings and are initially convex but later develop a central depression that may become funnel shaped; young, fresh caps tend to be more intense in color, with deeply in-rolled margins, and may be sticky to touch. The blue, crowded gills range from adnate to slightly decurrent, and the spore print is cream. The stems are typically central and slightly narrow at the base.

GROWTH

Commonly found after rain from summer to late fall, this widely distributed mycorrhizal species appears in deciduous and coniferous forests. It grows naturally in North and Central America, and occasionally in East Asia.

NOTES

This edible mushroom is sold fresh in rural markets in Central America and China, as it does not dry well. The desirability of this mushroom varies, with its slightly bitter to peppery taste and coarse, grainy texture dividing opinions. Its copious quantities of blue milk add color to marinades and sauces.

INDIGO MILKCAP

Lactarius indigo

LICHEN AGARIC

Lichenomphalia umbellifera

These pale mushrooms, which are one part of a lichen, partner with the green algal mat on the soil they live on. Found after rain, this inedible species has a wide geographic range and can pop up everywhere from tree trunks to damp soil. Growing solitarily or in groups, lichen agaric is an important partner for the green algae it forms a symbiotic union with.

APPEARANCE

These small, pale brown, frilly mushrooms have flat caps with a depressed center. The caps are smooth, dry, and waxy, ranging from buff to light orange-brown in color. The margins are translucent-striate with scalloped edges. The gills are decurrent, distant, and waxy cream to buff colored, and the spore print is white. The stems are relatively long, central, smooth, and cylindrical, often with pale, fuzzy mycelium at the base.

GROWTH

These lichenized mushrooms are the reproductive structures of the fungus partner that appear after rain. Found all year round, this species commonly grows on soils that are periodically damp, like roadsides and rotting wood. Even though this species is global in distribution (it has even been found on subpolar islands), it's rarely recorded in Africa or South America.

NOTES

This species is assumed to be non-poisonous. Although it often appears to be part of a mix of organisms in biological soil crusts, it has a symbiotic relationship with green algae; lichens are mutually beneficial symbioses between fungi and algae and/or cyanobacteria. The fungus mycelium helps hold the substrate together and shares water and micronutrients. In return, the algae partner shares sugars from photosynthesis.

You'll have to travel to South America to see these unique purple mushrooms, which are only found growing on the forest floors of Patagonia. The striking colors of this fungus make it quite easy to spot on the branches, logs, and soil on which it grows. If you're lucky enough to spot one while hiking, be sure to take a photo of its vivid magnificence.

APPEARANCE

These medium to large mushrooms have shiny, sticky caps, which become glutinous when wet and are convex (often with umbo); their colors range from lilac to pink-purple and violet. The gills are sinuate and begin life as a pale lilac before becoming rusty-brown with spores. The stems are central, even, pale near the gills, and sticky, with purple colorations below the cortina (cobweb-like ring), which is often rusty-brown with spores. With no particular odor, and with similar mushrooms found across the world, including in Patagonia, these mushrooms can be tricky to identify.

GROWTH

Found singly or in groups, Magellan's webcap are abundant after rain from March to June, depending on locality and season. Only found with trees living in the Nothofagaceae forests of Patagonia, these mushrooms have a highly restricted distribution.

NOTES

Although the species is considered edible, eating is not recommended, due to the high number of similar-looking species. These mushrooms play an important role within their ecosystem as mycorrhizal partners of other species present in the surviving Gondwanan forests of Patagonia.

MAGELLAN'S WEBCAP

Cortinarius magellanicus

MAGIC MUSHROOM

Psilocybe cubensis

This small, unassuming mushroom is the best-known hallucinogenic species, due to its wide distribution and ease of cultivation. Influential during the psychedelic period of popular culture (particularly within the music, art, and poetry scenes of the 1960s and '70s), this somewhat controversial fungus is commonly associated with research by psychologists during the period. Although research was halted for decades, magic mushrooms are back on the therapeutic agenda, with psilocybin treatments getting the go-ahead in Australia and parts of the United States.

APPEARANCE

The caps of these mushrooms are smooth, brown, and convex to conical, with a central pointed umbo, becoming broadly convex as they mature. The narrow, gray gills darken to purplish-black and appear somewhat mottled with age, but usually retain white edges. The spore print is dark purple-black. The stems are central and pale when young, turning brown with age. All parts of this mushroom may bruise blue with handling.

GROWTH

This pan-tropical to temperate decomposer species is associated with rich mulch, soil, and herbivore manure and is typically found after heavy rains.

NOTES

The active compounds of psilocybin and psilocin have been used by generations of Indigenous peoples, such as the Mazatec tribe of Oaxaca, who use magic mushrooms in healing ceremonies. Although the active compounds were widely criminalized in the past, recent scientific research has focused on their therapeutic potential for inclusion in supportive treatments for depression and anxiety.

These pretty, pale-apricot-colored mushrooms, also known as "salmon waxycaps" and "butter meadowcaps," can be found scattered through meadows and woods. While this mushroom is edible, some populations are in decline in Europe, so leaving this species undisturbed will increase its chances of survival. There are plenty of other wild mushrooms to collect that don't have the same conservation concerns, so best to leave this one in the ground where it belongs.

APPEARANCE

These medium-sized mushrooms have caps that are pale apricot in color; they are dry, smooth, convex, and broadly umbonate, with margins turning upturned and slightly wavy with age. The gills are decurrent, thick, broad, distant, and similarly colored to the cap; they may become deeper in color with age. The spore print is white. The stems are central, stout, and tapered toward the base. The existence of similar dry waxcap species mean this mushroom can be confused with others.

GROWTH

Found after rains from fall to spring, these mushrooms mainly grow in temperate grasslands in Europe and in woodlands throughout the east and west coasts of North America. The name has sometimes been used in Central America, West Asia, Australia, New Zealand, and South Africa, but those mushrooms are likely similar-looking species. Although this species has historically been considered a decomposer, recent research shows it may live biotrophically with bryophytes, such as mosses.

NOTES

This mushroom is generally considered to be edible, although it is not highly prized like some other culinary species.

MEADOW WAXCAP

Cuphophyllus pratensis

ORANGE MOSS AGARIC

Rickenella fibula

These tiny, bright orange, pin-like fungi stand out on the deep green mosses they inhabit. You'll find this common, moss-dwelling species, also known as "orange nail fungus" and "orange mosscap," growing everywhere from the United Kingdom to New Zealand, where it pops up after periods of rain. Due to diminutive size and inedibility, this fungus is left out of forager's baskets.

APPEARANCE

These small, orange fungi have very long stems and little odor or taste. The caps are dry, smooth, and convex or flat, with a central dot that is a raised or depressed dome; the dot is typically darker than the rest of the cap. The gills are decurrent and cream colored, and the spore print is white. The stems are slender, central, smooth, and tan or pale orange; they often has a slightly swollen base.

GROWTH

This species is found during wet seasons all around the world, but rarely in Africa. It is always associated with living mosses, with which it has a biotrophic relationship. To successfully conserve the orange moss agaric, its moss hosts need to be taken into consideration.

NOTES

The ecology of this pretty little fungus is just beginning to be discovered. Although the orange moss agaric looks like a mushroom, according to molecular analysis, the species is more closely related to certain other fungi. Beginners may mistake it for an orange chanterelle, but the orange moss agaric is not considered edible.

This small, bright orange, fan-shaped mushroom has become a weed, spreading across the world. Also known as the "orange ping pong bat" and the "orange pore conch," this invasive species threatens native fungi and alters ecosystems as it spreads. Help limit the reach of this fungus by only hiking with clean boots, hats, bags, and other possessions and by using pathogen hygiene stations while visiting national parks.

APPEARANCE

These very small, orange, fan-shaped mushrooms grow in clusters and have a gelatinous texture. The caps are usually flatly convex and attached laterally with short to long stems. The gills are modified into pores that are usually pentagonal to hexagonal but can be rounded. The stems are attached to the side of the cap and are cylindrical; they vary in length and sometimes appear wider at the base. This species complex is still being defined, with several new names. Other species from this genus that are indigenous to the areas they grow in are not as orange.

GROWTH

This decomposer is highly competitive in wetter areas across temperate, subtropical, and tropical zones. It reproduces prolifically after rain on wood of any size from the ground up into the canopy. Originally thought to be from Madagascar but with several new species centered in Asia, this species complex has spread across Australia, Africa, Asia, South America, Europe, and New Zealand. This weedy fungus is a threat to ecosystems, as it reduces the diversity of decomposers.

NOTES

There are no known uses for this weedy, inedible fungus, although it is a food source for slugs and snails. It is easily spread, so biosecurity hygiene should be practiced, particularly before visiting uninfected high-conservation-value areas.

ORANGE PORE FUNGUS

FUNGUS

Favolaschia claudopus

ORANGE
WAXCAP

Hygrocybe aurantiosplendens

These brightly colored mushrooms, which tend to grow in groups, are now rarely found across their range. This species is considered an indicator of a healthy environment, but as most populations of the orange waxcap are in decline, this mushroom is listed as endangered or vulnerable in many countries.

APPEARANCE

These mushrooms have sticky caps that are conical, smooth, and slimy when young, ranging from orange to bright red until they turn yellow with age. The gills are narrowly adnate, thick, waxy, and cream to yellow in color. The spore print is white. The stems are yellow or orange before tapering toward a white base; they are central, thick, dry, and smooth, sometimes with fine, longitudinal fibers.

GROWTH

Found in small groups after rain, these mushrooms peak in fall. The species mainly occurs in Europe, where it inhabits old, unimproved, calcium-rich grasslands, but it is also found in forests and woodlands in Siberia and North America. Although this mushroom has historically been considered a decomposer, recent research shows it may live biotrophically with bryophytes, such as mosses.

NOTES

This species is now very rare. An indicator of high-quality grasslands throughout Europe, this mushroom's protection is needed to prevent its extinction.

As one of the most popular culinary mushrooms, this common, fan-shaped species is grown around the world for food. While many choose to forage for the wild variety, oyster mushrooms are easily found at food markets and grocery stores. In recent years, it's become easier for home growers to cultivate this mushroom via grow kits containing sawdust, cottonseed hull, or recycled coffee grounds for it to flourish in.

APPEARANCE
These mushrooms grow in larger clusters with colors ranging from off-white to dark brown. The caps are dry, smooth, and convex, with in-rolled margins when young, which become lobed or wavy with age. The closely spaced gills are decurrent and colored white to off-white. The spore print is white, and the stems are often short, robust, and laterally attached, with firm, white flesh. The mushroom's bittersweet odor is reminiscent of almonds or anise.

GROWTH
These mushrooms reproduce all year round. As a primary decomposer of wood (especially deciduous trees – beech trees in particular), this species is widespread in temperate and subtropical forests throughout much of the world.

NOTES
Oyster mushrooms are among the most commonly sought species in the wild. They are best picked young, as they become tough and bitter with age. Considered a versatile culinary ingredient, oyster mushrooms are highly nutritionally beneficial, with compounds advantageous to heart health. Apart from being a food source, these mushrooms are used industrially as decontaminants.

OYSTER
MUSHROOM

Pleurotus ostreatus

PARROT
WAXCAP

Gliophorus psittacinus

These glossy mushrooms can hard to find in grass, their deep bottle-green blending in with their surroundings. As they age, however, parrot waxcaps become more colorful – their new shades of yelow, orange, and pink may be easier to spot. This species is uncommon, but don't be surprised to find them popping up in fields or other places in nature where pesticides haven't been used.

APPEARANCE

These small, slimy mushrooms start out as a deep, dark green and may become yellow, orange, pink, tawny, and olivaceous with age. As they dry, they become bright flesh-pink. The caps are conical to convex, often with an umbo. The thick, crowded gills are dark green when young, fading to orange-yellow. The spore print is white. The stems are central, thick, moist, sticky, and hollow.

GROWTH

These mushrooms can be found after rains, peaking from fall to spring, depending on locality. They are found in grasslands, woods, and roadsides in wetter parts of Europe, North and Central America, and certain parts of Australia and New Zealand. While this species has historically been considered a decomposer, recent research shows it may live biotrophically with bryophytes, such as mosses.

NOTES

This mushroom is not commonly eaten, due to its small size, sliminess, and conservation value; moreover, gastrointestinal upsets have been reported in some people. Its presence is an indicator of well-managed, healthy grasslands in Europe.

If you see a pop of pink at the farmers' market, then this oyster mushroom may be for sale. These colorful, tropical fungi could almost be mistaken for a bouquet of flowers with their beauty. Easily grown on sawdust and straw, this species is a hit with home growers who live in humid, hot regions. Even though this mushroom loses its vibrancy when cooked, it's still a prized culinary ingredient.

APPEARANCE

Clusters of these mushrooms have a ruffled appearance in a range of pink shades, from bright to faded. The caps are convex and dry, with a smooth texture, often possessing a scalloped or frilly margin, which is in-rolled in young specimens. The gills are decurrent and closely spaced and can be pale colored. The spore print is white. The stems are reduced, laterally attached, and asymmetric (or absent).

GROWTH

These decomposer mushrooms grow all year round in the tropics and subtropics, with peaks depending on rainfall and seasonal conditions. Naturally occuring in Oceania, Asia, and the Americas, this mushroom is now cultivated elsewhere by farmers, but has not yet escaped into the wild.

NOTES

With an almost meaty texture, pink oysters are deliciously umami-packed when cooked, but sour when raw. With a tougher texture, they are best well cooked (though you do lose their vibrant color). Since this species grows rapidly and on a wide range of organic materials, it is favored by gardeners.

PINK OYSTER MUSHROOM

Pleurotus djamor roseus

PYRAMID BUILDER LEPIDELLA

Amanita pyramidifera

This white mushroom's amazing conical warts certainly command attention. Found only in Australia and Asia, this peculiar-looking specimen is one of the easier mushrooms to identify, thanks to the tight pattern of conical adornments that cover its surface. While people don't hunt this species for food, it catches the eye of nature photographers, who love to capture this distinctive mushroom's unique appearance.

APPEARANCE

This mushroom's conspicuous, acutely conical warts make it stand out. The caps are white or cream, sometimes with a gray-brown tint. The gills are free, white to creamy, and crowded, and the spore print is white. The stems are central and white and have a ring that is small and often indistinct, or that may hang from the cap margin. The stems are covered in soft, white tufts, which are densest below the ring; there may also be bands of scales or warts below the ring, while the base is swollen.

GROWTH

This species can be found throughout the year, with a peak from January to May. A mycorrhizal partner of eucalypts and some rainforest trees, this mushroom grows in eastern Australia and possibly all the way to Malaysia.

NOTES

There are no recorded uses for this visually striking species. While its edibility or toxicity is unknown, the genus it belongs to contains the deadliest of mushrooms.

These large, delicious, orange mushrooms are a forager's favorite.
A species that has made its mark on the culinary world, the saffron
milkcap is especially popular in Spain, where it's served in a variety
of dishes. While it's a popular fungus with modern-day foodies,
a Roman fresco from Herculaneum appears to depict this species,
suggesting that the gastronomic merits of the saffron milkcap have
been known for many centuries.

APPEARANCE

Featuring concentric rings on the caps, this mushroom is orange all over
but may go green with age or damage from handling. The gills are shortly
decurrent, crowded, and bright orange. The spore print is white. The stems
are typically marked with a random sprinkling of shallow, bright orange pits,
especially near the base. Look for bright, carrot-colored milk that eventually
turns wine-red.

GROWTH

Abundant from fall to winter throughout temperate regions, this mushroom
is found with trees in coniferous forests and pine plantations. Originally from
the northern hemisphere, this species' many regional varieties have spread
across the world's coniferous plantations. It has not yet had a conservation
assessment but appears common.

NOTES

One of the best known and most delicious of the large, edible mushrooms,
the saffron milkcap goes well in hearty soups and creamy risottos, or sauteed
with garlic and served on toast. Younger specimens (recognized by a slightly
in-rolled cap margin) are better for eating, as slugs, snails, millipedes, and
other creepy-crawlies can be found lurking inside more mature specimens.

SAFFRON MILKCAP

Lactarius deliciosus

SHAGGY MANE

Coprinus comatus

These fast-growing, shaggy mushrooms aren't fussy about where they grow, so expect to see them flourishing everywhere from suburban gardens to urban parks and rural meadows. The gills liquify into black ink with age, so if you pick these mushrooms, eat them quickly, or you'll have a black mess on your hands. When you stumble across this species, you'll instantly see why its nickname is "lawyers wig" – its shaggy cap looks just like the traditional wigs barristers wear to court in some countries, like the United Kingdom and Australia.

APPEARANCE

These mushrooms have almost cylindrical, long caps that initially cover most of the stem. The caps start out dry and white, with white to brown-tipped scales. The gills are free and very crowded, with spores that start white, rapidly turning pink and then black as they mature; the gills liquify simultaneously during this process. The stems are central and thick and can be tall, but remain partially hidden by the long caps as the mushrooms mature. The flesh is white and mild to taste.

GROWTH

These mushrooms may appear after rain at any time of the year, but they have a significant fall peak and are most common in temperate regions. As a decomposer, the shaggy mane often pops up on lawns, pastures, gravel roads, and other disturbed areas. It is listed as imperiled in Canada and is considered introduced in Australia, Iceland, and New Zealand.

NOTES

When young and fresh, this mushroom is considered a choice edible; however, cooking, eating, and preserving need to occur within four to six hours of harvest, before it liquifies into a black, inky mess. The liquid, black spores have been used as temporary ink for writing.

While they may not be visually spectacular, these unassuming mushrooms are among the most popular edible fungi across the world. A common replacement for meat in vegan and vegetarian dishes, this hearty, woody ingredient is found in everything from ramen to bourguignon. A nutritional powerhouse packed with vitamins and minerals, the humble shiitake is a healthy option, whether you eat it cooked in a meal or turned into chips and enjoyed as a nourishing snack.

APPEARANCE

These medium-sized, tough mushrooms have distinct, slightly shaggy caps, which may have cracks; brown to tan, they are convex with fine, fibrous scales that are densest at the usually in-rolled margins. The gills are adnexed, shallow, close, and creamy to buff colored, with slightly uneven margins. The spore print is white, and the stems are central but often curved.

GROWTH

This species is native to warm, moist parts of East Asia and is grown commercially around the world. In the wild, shiitake grows on the rotting wood of broad-leafed trees, including shii and other chinquapins.

NOTES

These popular mushrooms are prevalent in East Asian dishes. High in fiber, B vitamins, and trace minerals, The most recent growing techniques came out of Japan in the 1980s, yet this species has a long cultivation history, with the oldest records dating back to 1209 CE. Avoid eating these mushrooms raw, as allergic dermatitis has been recorded as a rare reaction.

SHIITAKE

Lentinula edodes

SKYBLUE PINKGILL

Entoloma virescens

This eye-catching, bright blue mushroom is coveted by nature photographers. A rare sight in the wild, the intense cobalt hue of this slender-stemmed wonder makes it stand out on the forest floors it inhabits. Unfortunately, its allure has resulted in people trampling the areas where the mushroom grows, so tread lightly when searching for this blue beauty.

APPEARANCE

While these pointy mushrooms are often an intense sky-blue, some parts may discolor green. The caps are dry and conical, while the gills are adnexed and close. The stems are long, even, and central with shiny radial fibers that are longitudinally twisted; they may have fluffy basal mycelium. The spore print is pink.

GROWTH

This species is found from the tropics to temperate zones after rain. Assumed to be a decomposer, it grows among moss and litter. While thought to originate from East Asia, these mushrooms are commonly found in Australia but have also been spotted in Southern Africa and South America.

NOTES

This vibrant blue mushroom's toxicity is currently unknown, but the same genus contains toxic members, so it's best to steer clear from eating this one. There is much uncertainty around this species and similar blue mushrooms from New Zealand, Madagascar, and other islands, so genomic taxonomic work is needed.

Spectacular by name, spectacular by nature! Impressive clumps of these large, golden-orange mushrooms proliferate on tree stumps and logs. Sometimes colloquially named the "laughing gym" (or "jim"), these common, toxic mushrooms grow in Europe, South America, and Australasia, where they look especially resplendent when bathed in sunlight.

APPEARANCE

The caps are dry and initially convex with an in-rolled margin, which flattens with age but often retains a slight umbo; they can be gold to deep orange to orange-brown, often with orange-brown scales. The gills are crowded and adnate to sub-decurrent and start yellow to yellow-orange, then become rusty as the spores mature. The stems are central and thick, featuring a yellow and often reduced ring that is covered with rusty spores as the mushrooms mature. The lower stems are fibrous yellow to orange-brown above the ring and slightly swollen or bulbous below.

GROWTH

This mushroom is found throughout the year after rain, with fall as its peak season. As a decomposer, the spectacular rustgill typically grows on tree stumps, logs, or the bases of hardwoods and conifers. It is found in temperate forests and woodlands, but this species' wide distribution doesn't extend to North America.

NOTES

These mushrooms contain many compounds, including psychoactive compounds and neurotoxins. Consuming a spectacular rustgill may cause severe abdominal cramps and gastric upsets.

SPECTACULAR RUSTGILL

Gymnopilus junonius

SPLITGILL
MUSHROOM

Schizophyllum commune

It's easy to overlook this small mushroom, but take a peek underneath and you'll find distinctive gills that look like a flower in bloom. This unassuming mushroom is known for its mega-diversity of fertile pairings, with over 23,328 distinct mating types or "sexes." In recent years, the mushroom has piqued medicinal researchers' interest as a potential treatment for cancer, its compounds reported to have potential benefits in some therapy.

APPEARANCE

This tough, fan-shaped or pendulous mushroom has no stems and often appears in a shelf-like arrangement on wood. The small caps are covered with dull white to gray hairs. On the underside, the pale and distinctive divided gills are arranged radially from the point of attachment.

GROWTH

These common mushrooms are a truly global decomposer of wood, found on all continents except Antarctica. While they need moisture to reproduce opportunistically throughout the year, amazingly these mushrooms can remain dry for decades and then be revived with moisture.

NOTES

Long used in indigenous medicine, this species has recently attracted interest from medicinal researchers. However, take care – if inhaled, its spores can be harmful, particularly to people who are immunocompromised or prone to allergies.

The name of this mushroom hints that it has a trick up its sleeve. Its surprise? Underneath the unassuming, pale brown caps, you'll find vivid paprika-colored gills. This species is collected, not to be eaten, but for dyeing fabrics like wool and silk, as the rich hues of the gills create a natural alternative to synthetic dyes.

APPEARANCE

These medium-sized mushrooms have caps that are broadly umbonate and become flatter with age. The cap surface is dry and smooth to silky fibrillose, while the colors range from red-brown to umber-ochre, with a darker center. The gills are fairly crowded, adnate, and markedly sinuate, starting intensely blood-red, then becoming dull rusty-brown with spores. The stems are central, dry, smooth to silky fibrillose, and colored ochre to yellow-brown near the gills. The bases may have intensely paprika-colored mycelium. If you get close, you'll notice this mushroom emits a radish scent.

GROWTH

Appearing in the northern hemisphere during fall, this mycorrhizal species is mainly found alongside conifer and birch trees in North America and across Europe into western Russia. In some instances, these mushrooms can also be found under young spruce plantations on acidic soil.

NOTES

This mushroom is suspected of being toxic, as it may contain poisonous compounds present in similar pigmented species used for dyeing textiles.

SURPRISE
WEBCAP

Cortinarius semisanguineus

TROOPING CRUMBLE CAP

Coprinellus disseminatus

Sometimes called the "fairy inkcap," this small, gray mushroom can be found in clusters on tree stumps and roots all around the world. Often creating a dense carpet over the dead wood it grows on, this species is easily spotted because of the large congregations that bunch together. While it is considered non-toxic, foragers don't tend to seek this mushroom, due to its small size and tendency to fall apart if handled.

APPEARANCE

These small mushrooms start out pale with distinct dots on the caps' centers, becoming darker within hours as the dark spores rapidly mature; they begin as a pale white, gray or buff, darkening to gray or gray-brown. The caps are dry and conical to bell shaped. The gills are adnate, crowded, and white, turning gray and then black as the spores mature. The stems are white, thin, fragile, and smooth to minutely textured. The flesh is thin and brittle.

GROWTH

These mushrooms can be found at any time of the year after rain. They are a decomposer of wood, growing in masses on rotting tree stumps and roots. Widespread around the world from temperate to tropical regions, this mushroom is thought to be an introduced species in New Zealand.

NOTES

Reported to be edible, the species isn't highly regarded within the culinary world. Popular with time-lapse photographers (due to its ability to change quickly over time), this mushroom is different from many ink caps, as its gills do not liquify with age.

These unusually shaped mushrooms are known for their distinct golden web covering. They are only found in some corners of the United States; this relatively narrow distribution means you'll have to travel to specific forests in Oregon or California to see them. Since these mushrooms like to hide in the soil, they're not easily spotted, so you'll have to be committed to find them!

APPEARANCE

These mushrooms often have reduced stems and are characterized by a persistent golden membranous veil. The yellow or yellow-brown caps are dry, flat, and sometimes slightly depressed in the center. The gills are adnate to notched and appear whitish to yellow, browning as the spores mature. Stems are central and robust, appearing white with a golden partial veil. The basal mycelium is white.

GROWTH

This uncommon, medium-sized mushroom appears solitarily, scattered, or in small clusters. This species isn't spotted often, as it reproduces under duff or in soil, rarely becoming exposed. It appears from spring to summer (rarely in fall) with conifer and cedar trees. Considered a rare find, these mycorrhizal mushrooms only occur in mid- to high-elevation forests in the Sierra Nevada of California and the southern Cascade Range of California and Oregon.

NOTES

It's unknown if this species is edible, but consumption isn't recommended, as it is related to poisonous species.

VEILED
WEBCAP

Cortinarius verrucisporus

VELVET FOOT

Flammulina velutipes

These splendid, edible mushrooms with golden caps and dark feet are found in clusters on wood. Known as "velvet shank" in some parts of the world, this attractive species has many admirers, especially when the sunlight hits its cap. This mushroom isn't just a pretty face, though – its potential to combat cancer and other conditions is being investigated by the scientific community.

APPEARANCE

These small to medium-sized mushrooms have caps that begin as convex with in-rolled margins; once mature, they are convex or flat. Moist and sticky when fresh, the caps become dry, smooth, and shiny, with colors varying from dark orange-brown to golden-yellow-brown, often fading with maturity. The gills are sinuate and cream to pale yellow, becoming darker with age. The spore print is white. The stems are central and pale to yellow-brown to orange-brown near the gills. The stems darken toward the base and are covered with a dark, velvety coating.

GROWTH

Growing all year round, this mushroom peaks at different times depending on locality. It can be found in temperate Europe, North America, and Oceania. As a decomposer, it is mostly found on hardwoods, including on the buttresses of trees and shrubs, but it may also appear on woodchips.

NOTES

Less commonly eaten than their cultivated relative enokitake, these mushrooms are tougher but still tasty. Popular with photographers, the velvet foot is often found in shaded locations, the low light providing a challenge for cameras trying to capture the species' contrasting colors.

The rich, dark violet of this species lends it a distinctly gothic look. Violet webcaps are sought after by mushroom lovers, who are captivated by their unique hue. In some parts of the world, this dark beauty is getting harder and harder to find, so tread carefully to help this species continue to flourish in the future.

APPEARANCE

These medium-sized mushrooms are such a deep purple they may appear black in a dark forest. The caps are dry, convex, becoming umbonate to flat with age, and are covered in fine, downy scales. The gills are adnate and dark violet, becoming purple-brown with age. The stems are central, thick, and covered with wool-like fibrils, with swollen bases. Purple mycelium can also be present on the stem. Young specimens are sometimes covered in a cobweb-like veil. The spore print is rust colored, and the flesh is violet and darker at the margins. This species may have a cedar scent.

GROWTH

Found from late summer to early winter, this mycorrhizal mushroom peaks in fall. Predominantly found in conifer forests in North America and deciduous forests in Europe and Asia, this northern hemisphere species has occasionally been recorded in the southern hemisphere. In Canada, the violet webcap is considered imperiled, so consideration to help populations survive is recommended.

NOTES

Due to uncertainty with identification and the violet webcap's similarity to other species, eating these mushrooms is not recommended.

VIOLET
WEBCAP

Cortinarius violaceus

WAVY CAP

Psilocybe cyanescens

Commonly found in woody mulch, these "magic" mushrooms with psychoactive properties are subject to bans and regulations in many parts of the world. This means that growing, possessing, or selling wavy caps, known as the "blueleg brownie" in the United Kingdom, is likely prohibited, depending on where you live. Growing research into the potential benefits of psychoactive mushrooms may result in the species' future use in psychotherapy settings. Watch this space.

APPEARANCE
This small, brown mushroom can be tricky to recognize, but its cobweb-like ring and blue bruising are giveaways. Chestnut-brown when moist, the caps fade to pale buff or a yellowish color when dry. Mature caps are umbonate with wavy margins, while young specimens have conical caps. The gills start light brown and become purple-brown when mature, while the gill edges often appear paler. The central, dry stems range from off-white to buff, with a faint ring near the gills.

GROWTH
Found after heavy rains, this decomposer often appears in patchy clusters on woodchips in urban areas but also grows on other organic matter. It was originally found in the Pacific Northwest of North America, but its distribution rapidly expanded through humans' use of woody mulch. The species is now found across North America, West Asia, South Africa, Europe, and New Zealand.

NOTES
Identifying this species can be tricky, and unfortunately similar mushrooms have caused severe poisonings when eaten. Such identification difficulties can be solved through skilled cultivation. Despite this, many countries have banned or severely regulated the possession of these mushrooms, as they contain psilocybin and other alkaloids.

This very large, colorful, and delicious mushroom is easily cultivated in gardens. Considered to be a great replacement for meat, the wine-cap stropharia is fleshy with a mild, earthy flavor and is best picked and eaten when young. It it a perfect ingredient to add to sauces, soups, and dishes like risotto. If you try to grow these prolific mushrooms at home, you'll likely end up with an abundant supply.

APPEARANCE

This large mushroom's cap is usually burgundy in color and can grow to the size of a dinner plate; smooth and dry, they begin convex with in-rolled margins then become flat and cracked at the edges. The caps often have yellowy-cream patches. The crowded gills start off pale then turn gray as the spores mature, finally turning dark purple-brown. The stems are central, robust, and often thicker at the base, with a distinctive wrinkled ring, while the flesh is white.

GROWTH

This decomposer peaks in fall in temperate regions of both hemispheres. Originally found in North America and Europe, it has been introduced to gardens across Africa, South America, Asia, Australia, and New Zealand.

NOTES

This species is a favorite among mushrooms lovers for its nutty, earthy flavor. It is cultivated commercially, although it is illegal to grow or sell for consumption in Louisiana, United States. This species has a history of cultivation alongside corn in Europe, and recent studies confirm that it is an excellent growing companion for the crop, as it attacks problematic plant parasites.

WINE-CAP STROPHARIA

Stropharia rugosoannulata

WINE-COLORED AGARICUS

Agaricus subrutilescens

With a rich red-brown, fibrous cap and shaggy, white stem, this striking mushroom catches the eye in woodlands. While you may be tempted to collect this species due to its fruity fragrance, it's best left where you find it – you may end up with an upset stomach if you decide to eat it.

APPEARANCE

These large mushroom have convex caps, which become flat with age. Young specimens (and the center of mature specimens) are covered with dense, red-brown fibrils, with paler flesh underneath. The gills are fresh and begin white before turning pinkish, then dark brown with spores. The stems are central, often long, and tapered toward the gills; creamy-brown in color, they have pale, woolly scales below a skirt-like ring.

GROWTH

This species is mostly found in woods in late fall in North America and Central America. It is also found across South America, Europe, and Asia and has likely been introduced to Australia and New Zealand. Commonly found under redwood, pine, or alders, this decomposer prefers undisturbed habitats, which means it is likely becoming less common, though the species has not had its conservation status formally assessed.

NOTES

While considered inedible, this handsome mushroom is appealing to photographers.

This robust, often lilac-tinted mushroom is popular with foragers. While it is edible (and best enjoyed well done), the wood blewit is also used by crafters to dye textiles and paper. Known to sometimes grow in fairy rings, this delightful species is a wonderful example of the surprises you'll stumble upon in nature.

APPEARANCE

These medium to large mushrooms have a distinctive, sweet odor. The caps are smooth and convex with an in-rolled margin when young, becoming flatter as they age; they sometimes develop a broad umbo. Colors vary from lilac to pink-purple and pink-brown, dulling with maturity. The crowded gills are adnate (sometimes notched). The spore print is white to pale pink, and the stems are central and often enlarged toward the base. The basal mycelium ranges from white to lilac to purple, while the flesh ranges from purplish to lilac.

GROWTH

These decomposers are found after rain throughout the year, with a late summer to early winter production peak. They can be found in decaying leaf litter, coniferous and deciduous woodlands and plantations, grasslands, and some urban settings.

NOTES

These mushrooms are regarded as edible but have been known to cause allergic reactions, especially when consumed raw. Thanks to their strong flavor, they combine well with leeks and onions and can be preserved. This species has been cultivated for food in Britain, the Netherlands, and France, although cultivated wood blewits are said to be inferior in flavor to wild ones.

WOOD BLEWIT

Lepista nuda

YELLOWFOOT CHANTERELLE

Craterellus tubaeformis

Sometimes also called "winter chanterelles," these popular, edible mushrooms are often found in bountiful masses. With a stronger flavor than larger chanterelles, this gourmet species can be purchased from specialty produce stores and food markets when in season. Be sure to handle these delicate fungi carefully, as they damage easily.

APPEARANCE

These funnel-shaped mushrooms have contrasting dark brown caps and paler gills. The convex caps are often hollow down the middle, dry but waxy, and yellow to orangey-brown in color; their margins are often wavy and upturned. The gills are decurrent, shallow, and forked, and range from pale cream to light yellowy-orange. The spore print can range from cream to salmon-pink. The stems are central, hollow, smooth, and tapered toward the base, occurring in a range of colors from yellow to orange; they may become gray with age.

GROWTH

This species is found late in fall and often into winter, depending on the region, though they sometimes appear in late summer. Growing near trees and shrubs, these mycorrhizal mushrooms are currently found throughout North America and Europe, and occasionally in Asia, including Japan and Russia.

NOTES

When raw, these mushrooms have a distinctive, smoky, peppery taste, yet when cooked they possess a subtle, earthy flavor and firm texture. Beloved by gourmets, this chanterelle is easily dried for preservation. High in fiber, it contributes to the recommended intake of vitamins and minerals, including iron, potassium, phosphorous, thiamine, and vitamin D.

Many foragers have felt the pang of disappointment brought on by these mushrooms' telltale yellow stain. With a similar appearance to other species, yellow stainers are often mistaken for edible look-alikes, which is why they are frequently responsible for poisonings. Keep an eye out for a bright chrome-yellow that appears after handling – this is a warning sign that shouldn't be ignored.

APPEARANCE

These medium-sized mushrooms stain yellow and may have a slightly cube-like look and phenolic odor. The dry, smooth caps are initially convex, flattening as they mature; they are often white, with light brown tints toward the center, and may become scaly with age. The gills appear whitish, then pinkish, and finally dark brown as the spores mature. The stems are central and cylindrical, with an enlarged base that browns over time. Although the flesh may stain intense yellow, older, drier specimens may only stain at the stem base.

GROWTH

Appearing in abundance in fall (and after good rain in any season), this decomposer is found in grass, mulch, or litter in grasslands, parks, and woods. Considered native to Africa, North and South America, West Asia, and Europe, this species was likely introduced to Australia and New Zealand. Common in urban or disturbed habitats, these mushrooms may displace edible species.

NOTES

This mushroom is poisonous, causing sweating and stomach cramps. Its chemical odor becomes more obvious with cooking. Yellow stainers are likely to be a complex of species.

YELLOW STAINER

Agaricus xanthodermus

YELLOW UNICORN PINKGILL

Entoloma murrayi

This pretty yellow mushroom's pointy caps are behind its mythical unicorn name. Growing both solitarily and in groups, these dainty little wonders with long, thin stems pop up after rain like tiny umbrellas. This mushroom's magnetic charm ensures it's never short of admirers, with many photographers and artists keen to capture its beauty.

APPEARANCE

This mushroom's dry and smooth conical caps feature a distinct and sharply pointed umbo. The caps begin as bright yellow then fade with age. The gills are narrowly adnate and well spaced, with tidy short-gills. While the gills are yellow when young, they become pinkish with spores as they mature. The stems are long, hollow, slender, central, and smooth; they often have twisted, longitudinal striations, sometimes with a white mat of basal mycelium.

GROWTH

This species can be found from summer to fall after rainy periods, solitarily or in small groups. It mainly appears throughout temperate regions but sometimes apears in subtropical and tropical zones. This decomposer grows on wet ground among mosses, litter, and sometimes grasses and herbs in wet coniferous and deciduous forests. Most commonly found in eastern North America, it is also recorded in Central and South America and Southeast Asia.

NOTES

This mushroom is popular among nature photographers, but its toxicity is currently unknown, and it is therefore considered inedible.

These large, prominent mushrooms are a prized ingredient in Central Africa. This mushroom species may not be particularly well known around the world, but it's important to many people in Africa; the Zambian slender Caesar is a vital food source in the wet season, commonly sold at roadside food markets.

APPEARANCE

This large mushroom has a finely grooved ring and a broad sack with brown patches. The caps are spherical to egg shaped and olivaceous-brown in color but become flattened and paler with age; their surface is smooth and very sticky. The gills are free and white, with three tiers of short-gills. Gill edges may appear finely notched with a woolly texture. The central, relatively stout stems taper toward the gills.

GROWTH

This mushroom can be found solitarily or in small groups and is usually abundant at the start of the rainy season. Found in the Miombo woodlands of central Southern Africa, this species is most likely mycorrhizal with *Brachystegia* trees. Although an important food source, this species is not known to have been over-harvested. Despite this, the degradation of woodlands can cause localized extinctions.

NOTES

There are many local language names for this edible mushroom, which is popular in food markets. The plate-sized caps can be used as a pizza base, baked in a hot oven with your favorite toppings.

ZAMBIAN SLENDER CAESAR

Amanita zambiana

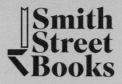

Published in 2024 by Smith Street Books
Naarm (Melbourne) | Australia
smithstreetbooks.com

ISBN: 978-1-9230-4901-7

Smith Street Books respectfully acknowledges the Wurundjeri
People of the Kulin Nation, who are the Traditional Owners of the
land on which we work, and we pay our respects to their Elders past
and present.

Publisher: Paul McNally
Editor: Avery Hayes
Design concept and layout: Olivia Bush
Illustrator: Marta Zafra
Proofreader: Penny Mansley

Printed & bound in China by C&C Offset Printing Co., Ltd.

Book 316
10 9 8 7 6 5 4 3 2 1